Water Goes Up!
Water Comes Down!

by Margie Burton, Cathy French, and Tammy Jones

Water is all around us.
Water is in the ocean.

Water is in the lakes
and rivers.

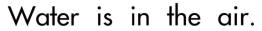

Water is in the air.

There is more water than land
on the Earth.

All things must have water
to live. The plants
must have it.

The animals
must have it.

We must have it, too.
We cannot live without
drinking water.

Sometimes, we do not have all the water that we need. This is what the land looks like when it needs water.

The land will dry up without water.

Sometimes, there can be too
much water on the land.
If it rains very, very hard,
the rainwater will run down
the hills. It takes some of
the land with it when
it runs down the hills.

It is called erosion when the water takes the land away.

All the water on the earth will never be used up. It goes from the ocean to the air to make clouds. Then, it falls from the clouds down to the land. It runs off the land and out to the ocean again.

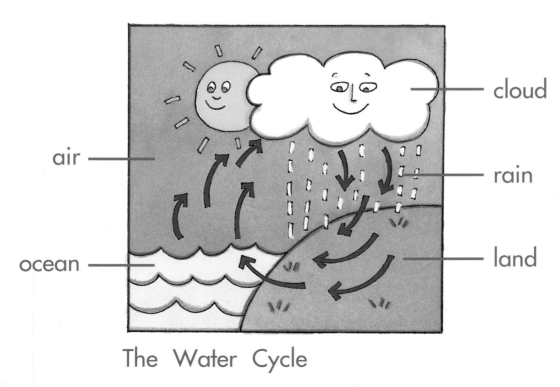

The Water Cycle

The clouds in the air
are made of water.

cirrus clouds

cumulus clouds

Sometimes the water falls down
from the clouds. It makes rain.

The rain falls onto the land.
Some of it goes into the ground.
Some of it washes down and
goes back into the ocean.

Some water falls down from the clouds that is not rain.

Some of this water is snow. The snow is made of water.

Some water that is not rain or snow falls down from the clouds.

Some of this water is sleet.
The sleet is made of water, too.

Sleet is made of little pieces of ice.

This also falls down from the clouds.
It is not rain or snow or sleet.

What do you think this hail is made of?

The water comes down from the clouds and goes back up again.

You can try this to see how the water can come down and go back up again.

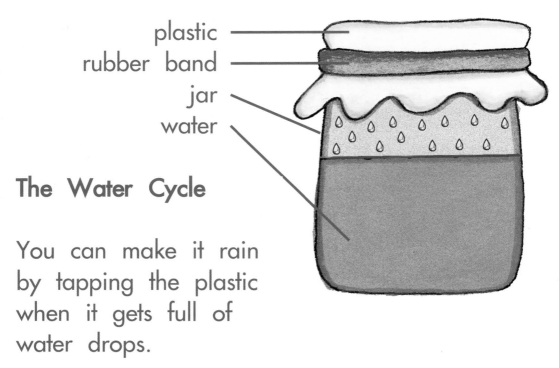

plastic
rubber band
jar
water

The Water Cycle

You can make it rain by tapping the plastic when it gets full of water drops.